T0394928

WASHINGTON COMMANDERS

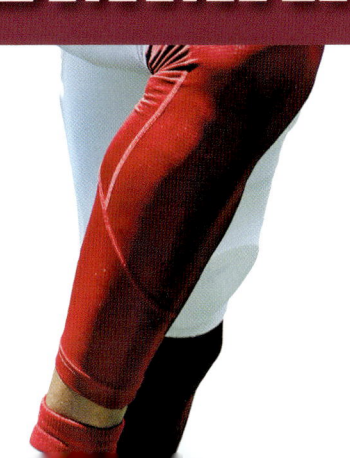

LUKE HANLON

Apex is distributed by North Star Editions:
sales@northstareditions.com | 888-417-0195

Produced for Apex by Red Line Editorial.

Photographs ©: Adam Hunger/AP Images, cover, 1; Rob Carr/Getty Images Sport/Getty Images, 4–5; Jess Rapfogel/Getty Images Sport/Getty Images, 6–7; Bettmann/Getty Images, 8–9; AP Images, 10–11, 12–13, 19, 20–21; Nate Fine/Getty Images Sport/Getty Images, 14–15, 24–25; Rick Stewart/ Getty Images Sport/Getty Images, 16–17; Paul Fine/Getty Images Sport/ Getty Images, 22–23; Wally McNamee/Corbis Historical/Getty Images, 26–27; Mitchell Layton/Getty Images Sport/Getty Images, 28–29; Ezra O. Shaw/Allsport/Getty Images Sport/Getty Images, 30–31; Jed Jacobsohn/ Getty Images Sport/Getty Images, 32–33; Mitchell Leff/Getty Images Sport/ Getty Images, 34–35; Focus On Sport/Getty Images Sport/Getty Images, 37, 52–53; Al Messerschmidt/AP Images, 38–39; Evan Vucci/AP Images, 40–41, 58–59; Patrick Smith/Getty Images Sport/Getty Images, 42–43; Cooper Neill/Getty Images Sport/Getty Images, 44–45; David Durochik/AP Images, 47, 57; Todd Olszewski/Getty Images Sport/Getty Images, 48–49; Ron Edmonds/AP Images, 50–51; Scott Taetsch/Getty Images Sport/Getty Images, 54–55

Library of Congress Control Number: 2024940177

ISBN
979-8-89250-162-0 (hardcover)
979-8-89250-179-8 (paperback)
979-8-89250-303-7 (ebook pdf)
979-8-89250-196-5 (hosted ebook)

Printed in the United States of America
Mankato, MN
012025

NOTE TO PARENTS AND EDUCATORS

Apex books are designed to build literacy skills in striving readers. Exciting, high-interest content attracts and holds readers' attention. The text is carefully leveled to allow students to achieve success quickly.

TABLE OF CONTENTS

CHAPTER 1

HAIL TO THE COMMANDERS

I t's a beautiful Sunday afternoon. Fans file into the Washington Commanders' stadium. The team is playing the Dallas Cowboys. Commanders fans always want their team to win. But they especially want to beat Dallas.

Washington Commanders receiver Jahan Dotson carries the ball in a January 2023 game.

The Commanders have the ball. Wide receiver Terry McLaurin cuts right. He loses his defender. Then he catches a pass and takes off. It's a touchdown! Washington's marching band begins to play. Fans sing along to "Hail to the Commanders."

LEFT HAND UP

In 2022, Commanders fan Woody Sellers made a music video. The song was about the team. It's simply called "Commanders Song." In the video, he puts his left hand up. It goes along with a line in the song. Soon, fans and some players adopted the slogan "Left Hand Up."

Terry McLaurin (17) celebrates after a touchdown catch in a January 2023 game against Dallas.

CHAPTER 2

EARLY HISTORY

The Washington Commanders have been playing since 1932. However, the team got its start in a different city. The team was originally known as the Boston Braves. In 1933, the team changed its name to the Redskins. The team remained in Boston, Massachusetts, for five years.

The team made one championship appearance during its time in Boston.

Boston reached the NFL championship game in 1936. But it lost to the Green Bay Packers. The next season, the team moved to Washington, DC. The team had instant success in its new city. Washington beat the Chicago Bears in the 1937 title game.

HISTORIC VENUE

From 1933 to 1936, Boston's football team played in Fenway Park. This baseball stadium was home to the Boston Red Sox. The Red Sox still play in Fenway Park today.

Washington quarterback Sammy Baugh (33) runs with the ball during the 1937 title game.

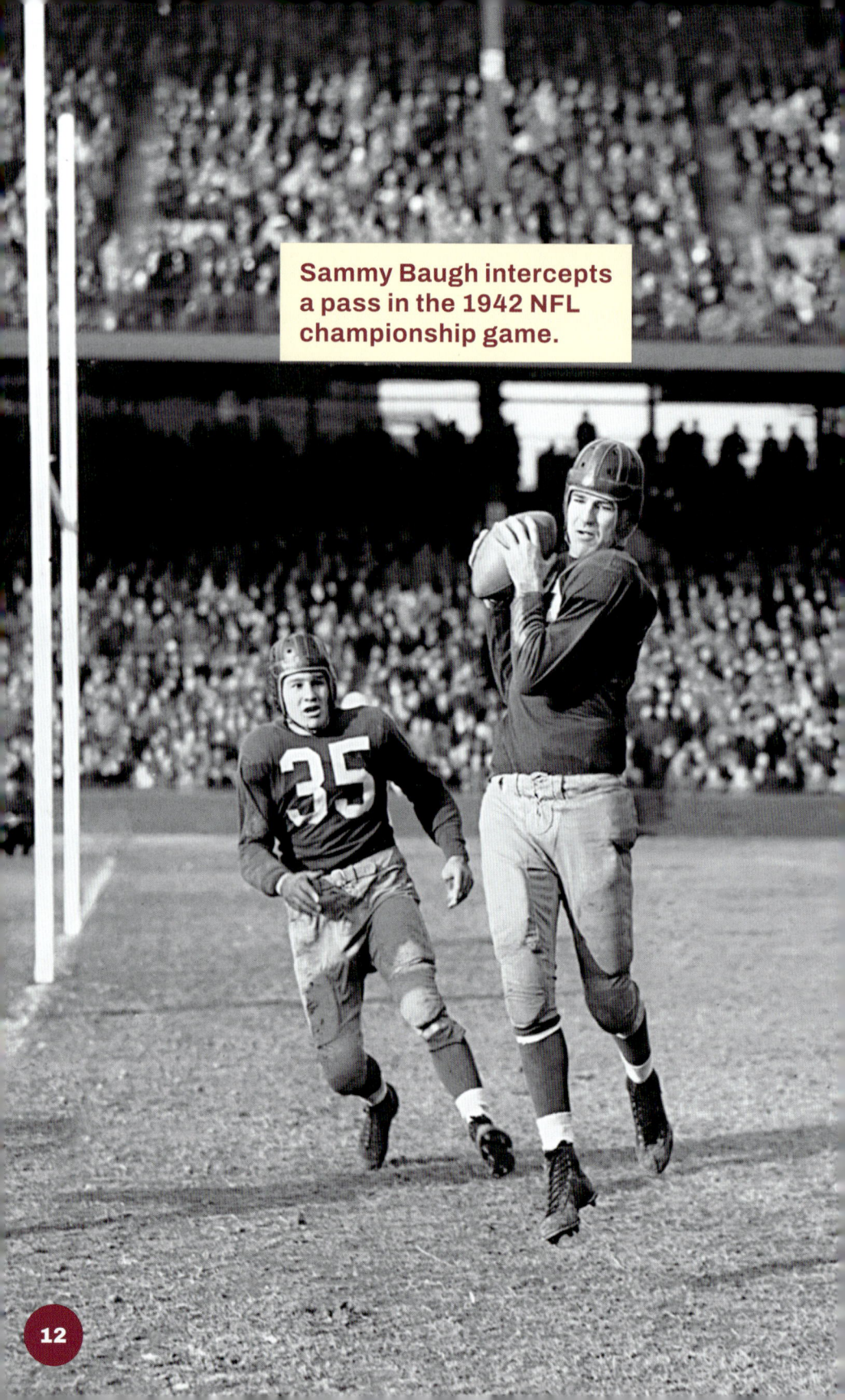

Sammy Baugh intercepts a pass in the 1942 NFL championship game.

From 1940 to 1945, Washington made four championship games. In 1940, the team faced the Bears again. Chicago crushed Washington 73–0. The two teams met again in 1942. Many fans expected a similar result. But Washington got revenge. It won the NFL title.

PROVEN WINNER

Ray Flaherty became Boston's head coach in 1936. He moved with the team in 1937. Flaherty coached Washington through the 1942 season. He led the team to two NFL titles. And he never coached a losing season with the team.

Washington struggled after 1945. The team missed the playoffs for years. Head coach George Allen helped turn things around. Washington hired him in 1971. In his seven years with the team, Allen led Washington to the playoffs five times.

FIRST SUPER BOWL

Washington reached its first Super Bowl in the 1972 season. However, the team faced a tough opponent. The Miami Dolphins entered the game with a 16–0 record. Washington fought hard. But the Dolphins finished their perfect season with a 14–7 win.

Quarterback Billy Kilmer (17) threw two touchdown passes in the 1972 conference title game.

In the 1987 season, Doug Williams (17) became the first Black quarterback to win the Super Bowl.

Washington hired Joe Gibbs as head coach in 1981. The team quickly became one of the NFL's best. By Gibbs's second season, Washington was back in the Super Bowl. This time, Washington beat Miami 27–17.

Gibbs led his team back to the Super Bowl three more times. Washington won two of them. In the 1987 season, Washington crushed the Denver Broncos 42–10. And in the 1991 season, Washington beat the Buffalo Bills 37–24.

SAMMY BAUGH

Washington drafted Sammy Baugh in 1937. It's no coincidence the team won the NFL title that season. Baugh helped Washington win another title in 1942. For 16 years, he did just about everything for Washington.

Baugh was an elite quarterback. He also carried the ball as a running back. Baugh played great defense, too. He finished his career with 31 interceptions. To top it all off, he even punted. One of Baugh's best years came in 1943. That season, he led the NFL in passing, punting, and interceptions.

SAMMY BAUGH JOINED THE PRO FOOTBALL HALL OF FAME IN 1963.

CHAPTER 3

LEGENDS

Passing was rare in the early days of the NFL. Then quarterback Sammy Baugh came along. He helped show the value of the forward pass. Washington still ran the ball, though. Cliff Battles was a big reason why. The running back led the league in rushing yards twice.

In 1933, Cliff Battles became the first NFL player to rush for more than 200 yards in one game.

Bobby Mitchell arrived in Washington in 1962. The wide receiver led the league in receiving yards that year. Then he did it again in 1963.

In 1964, Charley Taylor started out at running back. Taylor won the Rookie of the Year Award that season. He joined Mitchell as a receiver in 1966. Taylor led the league in catches that year. He led again in 1967.

Bobby Mitchell hauls in a pass during a 1967 game.

Chris Hanburger joined Washington in 1965. Little was expected of the linebacker. He was drafted in the 18th round. But Hanburger surprised the league. He turned into the leader of Washington's defense. Defensive back Ken Houston helped the team, too. He intercepted 24 passes. He also recovered 10 fumbles.

QUARTERBACK GREATNESS

Washington has been home to several great quarterbacks. Sonny Jurgensen had a Hall of Fame career. Joe Theismann won the Super Bowl in 1982. Then he won the Most Valuable Player (MVP) Award in 1983. Doug Williams and Mark Rypien had some great seasons, too. They led the team to its next two titles. Both won the Super Bowl MVP Award.

Chris Hanburger made nine Pro Bowls with Washington.

John Riggins was a bruising running back. He starred in Washington's first Super Bowl win. He earned the Super Bowl MVP Award. Washington's quarterbacks relied on Art Monk for years. The wide receiver ended his career after the 1995 season. At the time, he had the second-most catches in NFL history.

THE HOGS

Washington's Super Bowl offenses had many stars. But the biggest stars may have been the offensive linemen. The physical group earned the nickname "The Hogs." Several linemen made up the group over the years. They included Jeff Bostic, Russ Grimm, and Joe Jacoby. These three played in three Super Bowl wins.

John Riggins (44) ran for 166 yards and a touchdown during Washington's first Super Bowl win.

CHAPTER 4

RECENT HISTORY

Joe Gibbs coached another winning season in 1992. Washington went 9–7. Then the team won a playoff game. However, Gibbs left Washington after that season. He wanted to spend more time with his family.

In 1992, linebacker Wilber Marshall was one of Washington's top players.

Losing Gibbs was
a blow to the team.
Washington missed the
playoffs for six straight
years.

But in 1999, the team
was back. Washington
went 10–6 to win
its division. Then it
beat the Detroit Lions
easily in the playoffs.
Washington faced the
Tampa Bay Buccaneers
in the next round.
And it led 13–0 in
the second half. But
Washington gave up the
lead in a tough loss.

Quarterback Brad Johnson (14) led Washington to its return to the playoffs in 1999.

Running back Clinton Portis (26) was an offensive force during Joe Gibbs's return to Washington.

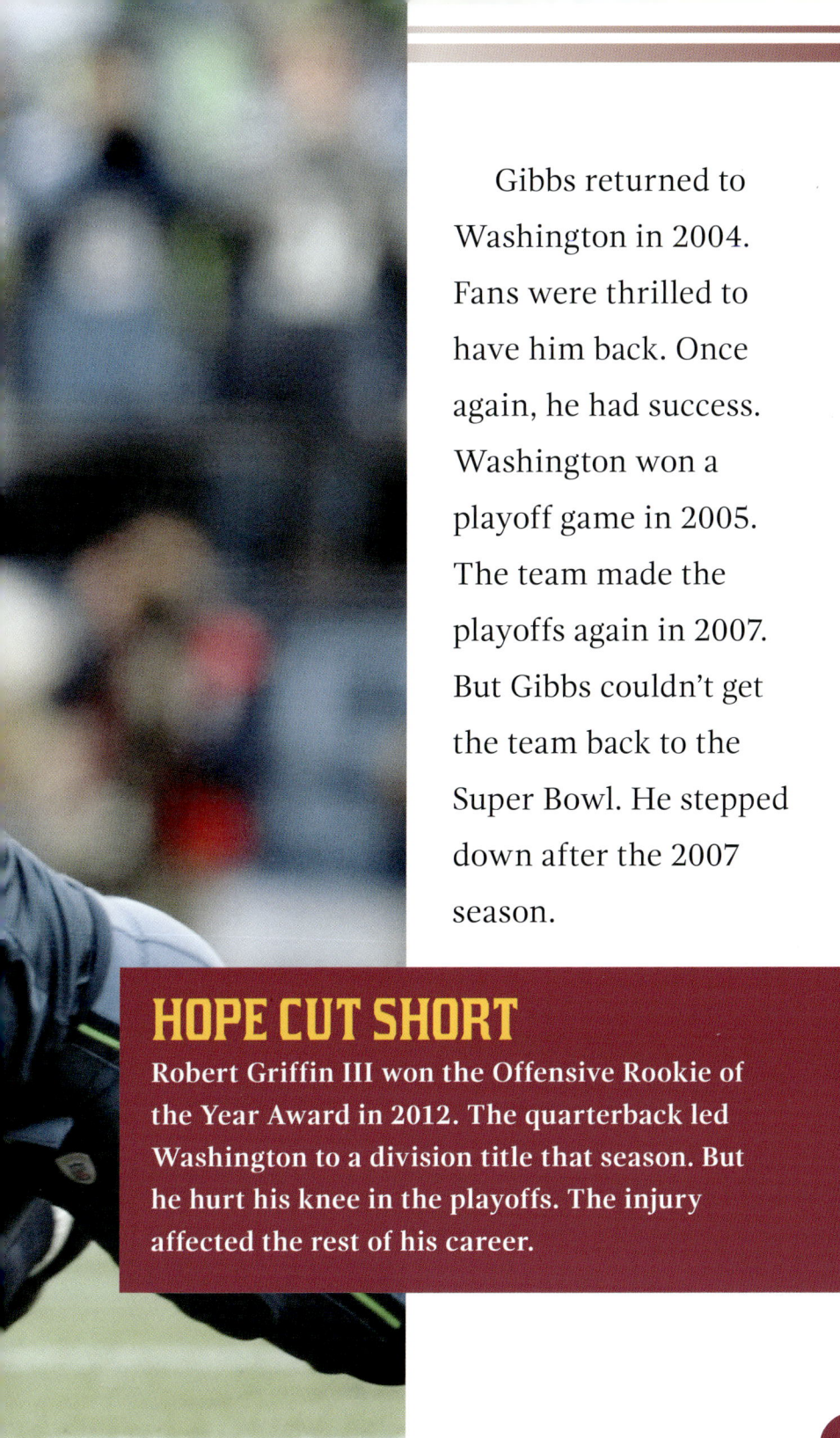

Gibbs returned to Washington in 2004. Fans were thrilled to have him back. Once again, he had success. Washington won a playoff game in 2005. The team made the playoffs again in 2007. But Gibbs couldn't get the team back to the Super Bowl. He stepped down after the 2007 season.

HOPE CUT SHORT

Robert Griffin III won the Offensive Rookie of the Year Award in 2012. The quarterback led Washington to a division title that season. But he hurt his knee in the playoffs. The injury affected the rest of his career.

Washington quarterback Alex Smith (11) earned the Comeback Player of the Year Award in 2020. He'd returned as a starter after breaking his leg in 2018.

Washington struggled to replace Gibbs. Some coaches had a good season or two. But none won consistently. From 2012 to 2020, Washington won its division three times. But each time, the team lost its first playoff game.

In 2024, Washington drafted quarterback Jayden Daniels. Fans hoped he could lead the team back to glory.

TIME FOR A CHANGE

For decades, many people wanted Washington to change its team name. It was a racist slur against Indigenous people. In 2020, the team finally dropped the name. It became the Washington Football Team. Then in 2022, the team started using the name Commanders.

JOE GIBBS

Joe Gibbs was voted into the Pro Football Hall of Fame in 1996. At the time, only two coaches had a better winning percentage than he did. Gibbs also had success in the playoffs. Going into 2024, Washington had won 23 playoff games. Gibbs led the team in 17 of those games.

Many great coaches have depended on one Hall of Fame quarterback. But Gibbs could turn just about any team into a winner. His three Super Bowl wins are proof. A different quarterback started each of those games. No other coach has ever done that. And none of those three quarterbacks were Hall of Famers.

JOE GIBBS COACHED WASHINGTON ACROSS 16 SEASONS.

CHAPTER 5

MODERN STARS

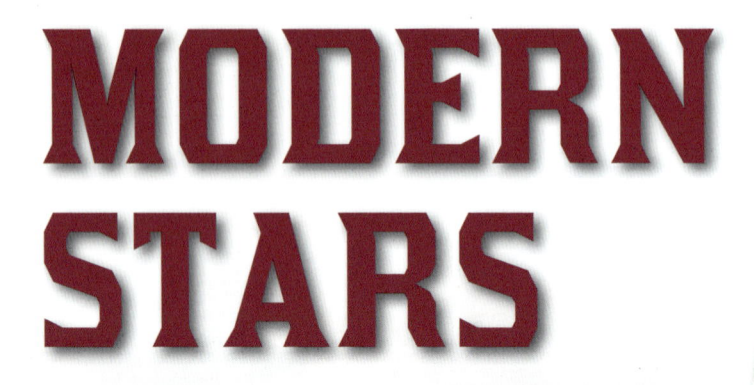

Darrell Green played for Washington his entire career. Green wasn't just a great defensive back. He was also a strong punt returner. Green made seven Pro Bowls between 1984 and 1997.

Darrell Green (28) returns a punt during a game against the Dallas Cowboys.

Linebacker LaVar Arrington put fear into his opponents. His hard hits caused fumbles. And he could take down quarterbacks. London Fletcher arrived a couple years after Arrington left. The linebacker often got the stop on defense. His 166 tackles led the NFL in 2011.

ONE STAR, THEN ANOTHER

Champ Bailey joined Washington in 1999. The defensive back excelled through the early 2000s. The team then traded him to Denver. Washington got running back Clinton Portis in return. Portis topped 1,000 rushing yards four times with Washington.

LaVar Arrington celebrates a tackle during a 2005 game.

Washington traded for Santana Moss in 2005. He was a reliable wide receiver for a decade. The team found another in 2019. Terry McLaurin used his great footwork to get open. In 2023, he recorded his fourth straight season with more than 1,000 receiving yards.

TRAGIC LOSS

In the 2000s, Sean Taylor was one of the best defensive backs in the league. His hard-hitting style earned him two trips to the Pro Bowl. Sadly, Taylor's life was cut short. He was killed in 2007. He was just 24 years old.

Santana Moss (89) dives for a touchdown during a 2012 game against the Philadelphia Eagles.

Ryan Kerrigan lived in the backfield. The star defender racked up sacks. And he often tackled running backs for losses. Kerrigan made four Pro Bowls in his career.

Washington added to its defensive line in 2017. The team drafted Jonathan Allen in the first round. Then in 2018, Washington took Daron Payne in the first round. The duo had played together in college. They continued to have success in the NFL.

Jonathan Allen (93) pressures the Houston Texans' quarterback in a 2022 game.

DARRELL GREEN

Darrell Green was known for his speed. The defensive back was one of the fastest players in NFL history. Green chased down players to stop touchdowns.

Green picked off many passes, too. He finished his career with 54 interceptions. That was a team record. Green also used his speed to score defensive touchdowns. He scored eight of them during his career.

Green played with Washington for 20 years. He had at least one pick in each of his first 19 seasons.

DARRELL GREEN HAD 621 INTERCEPTION RETURN YARDS IN HIS CAREER.

CHAPTER 6

TEAM TRIVIA

From 1961 to 1996, Washington played its home games in Washington, DC. The team opened a new stadium in 1997. It was located in nearby Landover, Maryland.

Washington's stadium has changed over time. In 2010, it could seat more than 90,000 fans. In 2024, its capacity was fewer than 70,000.

Across 1981 and 1982, Mark Moseley (3) kicked 23 field goals in a row. That was an NFL record at the time.

Mark Moseley could do no wrong in 1982. The kicker made his first 20 field goals of the season. And a few of them were game winners. Moseley won the league's MVP Award that year. He's the only kicker ever to win the award.

BALL HAWK

DeAngelo Hall made history in 2010. The defensive back intercepted four passes in one game. That tied an NFL record. Plus, all four of Hall's picks came in the second half.

The Dallas Cowboys are Washington's biggest rival. The rivalry started before the Cowboys even played their first game. Dallas was trying to join the league in 1960. But it needed a unanimous vote. Washington's owner voted to keep the Cowboys out. So, the Dallas owner responded. He bought the rights to Washington's fight song. To get the song back, Washington changed its vote. It let the Cowboys in. The teams have played twice a season nearly every year since 1961.

In the 1982 season, John Riggins (44) scored two touchdowns in a playoff game against the Cowboys.

In 2022, the Commanders needed a new mascot. The mascot had to match the team's new name. That's how "Major Tuddy" came to be. He is a pig that wears an army helmet. The helmet represents the team's new name. And the pig reminds fans of the Hogs of the 1980s.

REVIVING A TRADITION

A marching band started playing at Washington's games in 1937. It is the oldest marching band in the NFL. The band didn't perform at games in 2020 or 2021. That was because of the COVID-19 pandemic. The band came back for the 2022 season.

Major Tuddy takes the field with players before a 2023 game.

TEAM RECORDS

All-Time Passing Yards: 25,206
Joe Theismann (1974–85)

All-Time Touchdown Passes: 187
Sammy Baugh (1937–52)

All-Time Rushing Yards: 7,472
John Riggins (1976–79, 1981–85)

All-Time Receiving Yards: 12,026
Art Monk (1980–93)

All-Time Interceptions: 54
Darrell Green (1983–2002)

All-Time Sacks: 97*
Dexter Manley (1981–89)

All-Time Scoring: 1,206
Mark Moseley (1974–86)

All-Time Coaching Wins: 154
Joe Gibbs (1981–92, 2004–07)

NFL Titles: 2
(1937, 1942)

Super Bowl Titles: 3
(1982, 1987, 1991)

Sacks were not an official statistic until 1982. However, researchers have studied old games to determine sacks dating back to 1960.

All statistics are accurate through 2023.

TIMELINE

1932   **1937**   **1942**   **1972**   **1981**

The Boston Braves play their first NFL season.

Ray Flaherty leads Washington to its second NFL title.

Washington hires Joe Gibbs as head coach.

The team moves to Washington and wins the NFL championship.

George Allen helps Washington make its first Super Bowl appearance.

1982

1987

1991

2004

2022

Doug Williams throws for 340 yards and four touchdowns to win the Super Bowl MVP Award.

Washington rehires Gibbs after an 11-year break from coaching.

In his second season with the team, Gibbs leads Washington to its first Super Bowl win.

Gibbs wins his third Super Bowl with his third different quarterback.

The team changes its name to the Commanders.

COMPREHENSION QUESTIONS

Write your answers on a separate piece of paper.

1. Write a paragraph that explains the main ideas of Chapter 4.

2. Who do you think was the greatest player in Washington history? Why?

3. What quarterback led Washington to NFL titles in 1937 and 1942?

    A. Sammy Baugh
    B. Sonny Jurgensen
    C. Joe Theismann

4. How was Chris Hanburger's leadership a surprise?

    A. He ended up playing offense.
    B. He was picked very late in the draft.
    C. He played for only a couple of years.

5. What does **consistently** mean in this book?

Some coaches had a good season or two. But none won ***consistently.***

    A. never

    B. steadily

    C. rarely

6. What does **revenge** mean in this book?

Chicago crushed Washington 73–0. The two teams met again in 1942. Many fans expected a similar result. But Washington got ***revenge.*** *It won the NFL title.*

    A. a game that a team can't win

    B. the same result as a previous game

    C. a win by a team that lost earlier

Answer key on page 64.

GLOSSARY

backfield
The area of the field behind the line of scrimmage.

division
In the NFL, a group of teams that make up part of a conference.

fumbles
Plays when an offensive player loses possession of the ball.

Indigenous
Related to the original people who lived in an area.

interceptions
Passes that are caught by a defensive player.

pandemic
A time when a disease spreads quickly around the world.

rival
The opponent that a team has the most intense competition against.

rookie
An athlete in his or her first year as a professional player.

sacks
Plays that happen when a defender tackles the quarterback before he can throw the ball.

unanimous
Having agreement from all voters.

TO LEARN MORE

BOOKS

Anderson, Josh. *Inside the Washington Commanders.* Minneapolis: Lerner Publications, 2024.

Coleman, Ted. *Washington Football Team All-Time Greats.* Mendota Heights, MN: Press Box Books, 2022.

Whiting, Jim. *The Story of the Washington Commanders.* Mankato, MN: Creative Education, 2025.

ONLINE RESOURCES

Visit **www.apexeditions.com** to find links and resources related to this title.

ABOUT THE AUTHOR

Luke Hanlon is a sportswriter, editor, and author based in Minneapolis. He watches NFL games all day on Sundays during the fall.

INDEX

ANSWER KEY:
1. Answers will vary; 2. Answers will vary; 3. A; 4. B; 5. B; 6. C